Orange and Purple Skies

A poetry collection of friendship, love and relationships

Ekta Mourya

BookLeaf
Publishing

India | USA | UK

Presentation by *BookLeaf Publishing*

Web: www.bookleafpub.com

E-mail: info@bookleafpub.com

ISBN: 9789363312418

First edition 2024

For Neil

ACKNOWLEDGEMENT

I'd like to thank my mother for being my first and forever muse and my guiding light. A big thanks to my warm, kind and mostly funny friends, acquaintances.

PREFACE

Poems on the subjects of friendship, love and relationships, written at different times and different places. The poems in this collection may take you back to the corridors of your alma mater or remind you of the first date with your partner. The collection ages and gains character as I did, through my twenties and I hope your attention is nourished and your heart is warmer as you flip through the pages.

The works in this collection have featured in my personal communication with friends and lovers alike. The poems are inspired by the smallest act of kindness and the grandest gestures of love.

Find Ekta's poetry on Instagram:

@ektamouryapoetry

A broken heart or a broken clock, which is it?

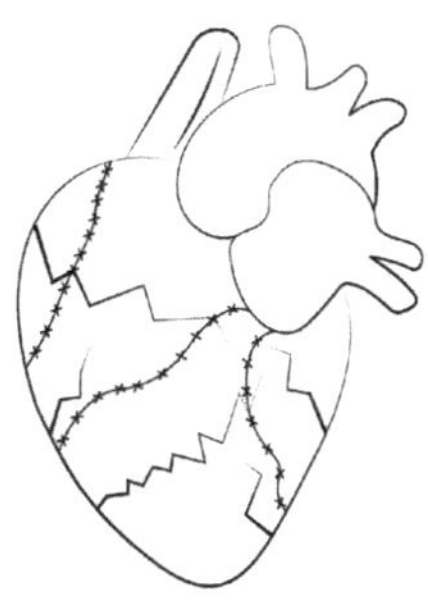

We have love
We have time
Do we have one or both?
The heart grows fonder, the farther you stay
They say
But do they know
The slow and painful passage of time
When it is spent away from the object of
affection
Of carnal desires
The muse, the lover
The inspiration, a burning flame
I call you by many names
Put time and space between us
You slip out of my hands like sand slipping
through my fingers

The heart races when anxious
In an attempt to bridge the distance
It calls out to you
In the silence of a night so long
Sleep grows weary
A broken heart
Or a broken clock
Which one is it?
Will we know?
The burning embers cooled long ago
It rained fires when you were gone
I sit in a pile of ashes now
With pieces of a broken heart.

A poem of love

I wanted to write you
A poem of love

One that speaks of birds
The vast ocean and its waves
The Orange and Purple Skies
And giant whales.

You'd wonder
What these natural wonders have to do
And how they relate to you.

The freedom of fearless flight
The wind in the wings of a kite
The light that peers through its wings
Is reminiscent of how I soar

Of how your love pushes me to fly
Spread my wings in the sky.

The Orange and Purple Skies
Are reminders
Of the hues that my heart takes
When it's flooded with passion
With love and delight.

The giant whales
That forage, migrate, mate and explore
The vast seas
Represent
Everything I want for you and me.

This is a poem
Of a love that cannot
Be outdone
Or outlived
Or forgotten

It burns slowly
Like a fire
Hopeful and warm
On a cold winter's night

For you and I
Are made of stardust
Part mortal

Part celestial

Experiences you may have many
But the love we share
Permeates every vibration of your being
And travels beyond time and space
Pushes past the barriers of dimensions
And stays with you lifetimes and lightyears
away

Keeping you warm
On a cold floating ball of life
On a cold winter's night.

Falling stars

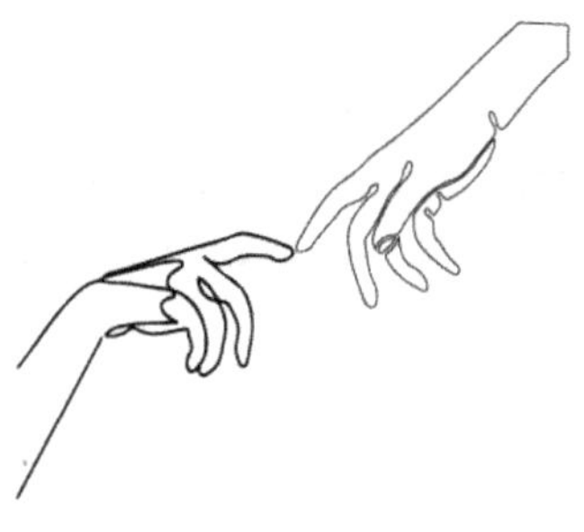

A falling star
Carries the baggage
Of countless wishes
Of stories untold
Stare at it, in the abyss of the night
You'll see
It still burns brightly
Right until the end
Till its shine is lost
To fulfilling the dreams
Of millions.

I would find you again and again

There's a strange beauty
In thinking about you
I feel a spark ignite, inside my heart
When I think of you
I hear your voice in my head
Every word you ever said
It's like you live inside me
And I continue loving you
Just how I love myself
I love you again and again, every day
You make me melt
You make me cry
You make me miss you
Till my tears are dry
But you make it worth my while
I may say a million mean things

But I don't mean harm
I just want you to be the best version of yourself
To live your life on your terms
To fulfill your potential
Because you are my inspiration and my muse
Even if we existed in a different time or a
different life
Even if we were separated by distance
If I was light years away from you
I know I would turn around
Look for you
And I would find you
Again and again.

The beautiful moon

Look at the beautiful moon
Have you ever wondered what makes it shine so
bright?
Who gives it the light?
Why is it the God of the night?
The sun makes the moon shine
Like you make me shine brighter everyday

Look at the giant waves of the sea
Have you ever wondered what makes them so
mighty and grand?
What gives water the strength
Of a million strong men?
The moon does it
Like you inspire strength and courage in my
heart

Look at my smile
Have you ever wondered what makes the
corners of my eyes light up?
What makes me blush, what makes my face
glow?
You do it
Like the sun and the moon
You make life in this cold dark universe
Worth my while.

Baggage

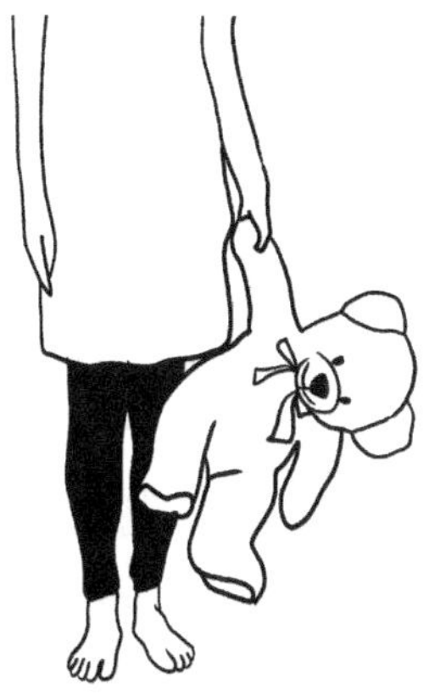

When everyone brought baggage
You came empty-handed
When everyone left
You stayed behind
The noise and the party was over
The night and its silence arrived
You held me
From a distance
From across the room
I locked eyes with you
Letting you closer
Than anyone had ever come
And thus it began
From a sea of strangers
To the one who feels like home.

Three and a half months

Three and a half long months
I've struggled to find the words to describe
How the thought of you makes me feel
There aren't enough words
And if there are words
They aren't exactly right
This is one of those things in life
That you seal with a kiss on the lips and not a
response
I see time passing by
I feel the pain in the hollow of my chest
The gaping hole from missing you for a hundred
days and a hundred nights
You may feel that I run away from you
I run from love that is so real, that it hurts

I don't run away because I don't want you
I run away from the pain
Of the three and half months
Of the realization that I've never wanted
anything more
Than to hold
And be held
By my lover and my muse
My home
In a sea of strangers.

Missing

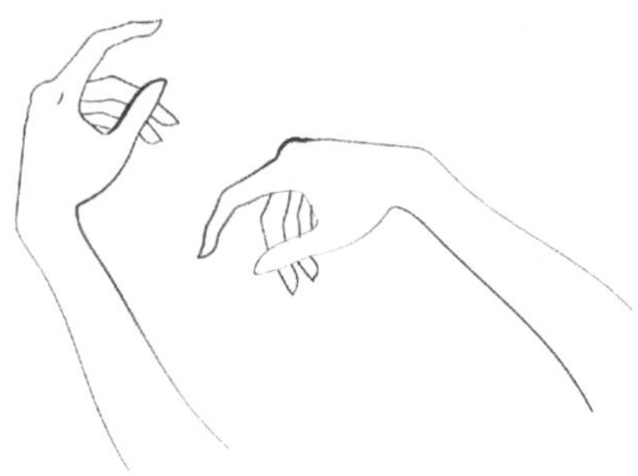

Missing the thrill of a name flashing across your
phone screen
The phone call that could turn a bad day into a
good one
Missing someone to the extent that you feel
physical pain
And at the same time holding yourself back,
hiding your true feelings
And convincing yourself and them
That you are just friends
The inner battle
Is intense
It is raw and real
But missing doesn't cut close to describing
The pain that floods your insides
The pain you process
Through parties and noise
Through strangers in crowded clubs

You hit rock bottom
But you know
You are missing...

Stand still

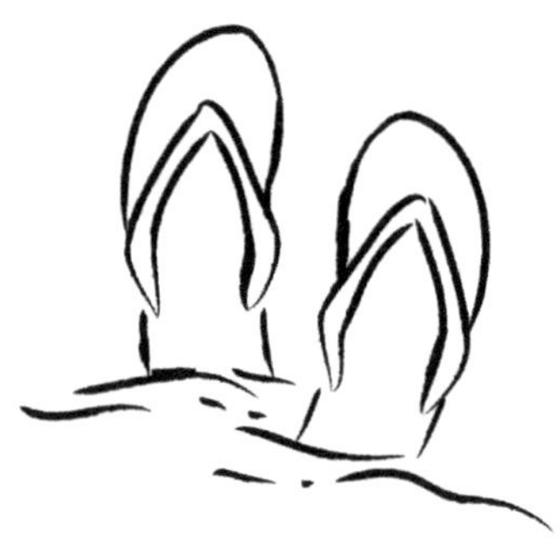

You stand still
As time passes
You watch seasons change
You stand still through your classes
The parties and the games
You stand still
And you want to hit pause on it all
Your racing thoughts
The passage of time
You want to turn inward
And shut everyone and everything out
You don't want to deal with the absence
Of the one you are missing
Of your home
In a sea of strangers.

A song stuck in my head

Playing your voice in my head
A million times a day
Playing it on repeat, like a beautiful melody
It doesn't matter if you are
A million miles away
You are a song
A song stuck in my head
When I'm walking down the street
When I'm daydreaming
Writing, thinking or creating
Why won't you leave
Aren't you tired of traversing the roads of my
mind
Just like a song stuck in my head.

Sweet friend

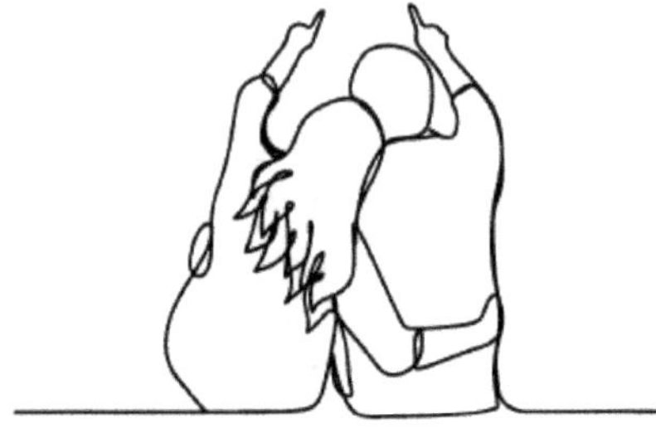

Don't let them break your spirit
With their criticism and judgment
Keep your passion burning bright
Keep up the good fight
Sweet friend
It is a gift to dream
To break the curse of the lemmings
To stand up tall and proud
Have a voice in the room
Pull a chair
It is time you made your voice heard.

Orange and Purple Skies

When I say I love long winter nights
It's not the cold that draws me in
It's the anticipation and the wait for the warm
sunshine
That draws me in
Like a moth to bright lights
When I say I love a walk on the beach
It's not the sand and the sea that I like
It's the warmth of the hand I hold, the comfort of
the voice in my ear
The promise of another date and another night
That draws me in
Like a moth to bright lights
When I say I love the sunset
It is not the setting sun or the dimming light that
lures me in

It is the Orange and Purple Skies
The way the day melts slowly into the night
That draws me in
Like a moth to bright lights.

Heart break

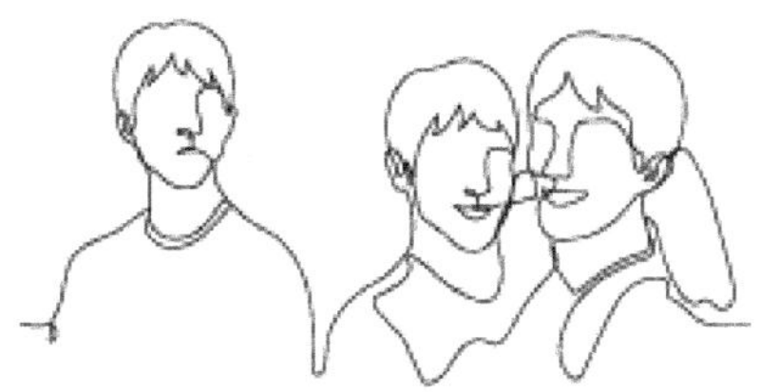

Does the moon's heart break
When she sees the one I hold dear
Is far
Is miles away
We are separated by the cycle of night and day
Will she call out to you
When you look at the sky
Will she tell you that the heartbreak
Broke my insides
That she counts every tear
I shed in the night
Does the moon's heart break
To see us apart
When promises were made
And you held my heart
Does the moon's heart break
When she sees you again
With a new face by your side, smiling at her
Does the moon's heart break
When she sees me waiting for your return
Writing poetry for you
Telling her, that you are the one.

With you

I close my eyes
Screaming at the world outside
Holding on to the memories tightly
Feeling the rain on my skin
It washes away the dreams of seeing you
I wish I could touch your face
Make you laugh again
Watch that smile
Fight over silly things
Stay up all night
Death did us part
Before we could set it right
Wish I could find my way to your world
And buy some time
Spend it dancing with you
Hold you in the rain
Kiss you goodbye…

Strangers

Do they like talking
Or is it too personal for their taste
Why did they disappear?
Why did they give up anyway?
Said you feel too much
You are an empath
Why didn't that stop them from feeding on your
love
Why didn't that stop them from coming back
Maybe if you stepped away
You'd be alright
In another world, another time
You'd be friends, lovers or enemies
Maybe you would be anything
But strangers.

Who feels like home in a sea of strangers

The heartbreak may have been painful
The good times were probably worth your while
Loving someone cuts you deep
Now swiping left and right
Sharing intimacy like it was a piece of bread
Go back to the writing board
Think back to the times
You'd hold one hand instead of twenty
You'd write a letter
Not send a reel
You'd wish every date was longer
You'd spend hours on call every night
Who was your island
In a sea of strangers
Who silenced your demons
Embraced your inner child
By now you've thought of the person
So many times that you know

Who feels like home
In a sea of strangers.

25

Did you break me

I don't think of you
Every waking moment of my life anymore
I have pieced together
My once-broken heart
I don't feel the hollow in my chest
That pained in your absence
And made me scream at night
I have replaced you with demons
That don't let me see what is wrong from right
I run away from promises, commitment and
labels
Did I heal or did you break me?

Safe place

I hurt someone who filled my cup till his was
empty
I hurt a lover and a friend
I hurt him over and over again
It reminded me of the hurt you caused
I can't forgive you
Nor can I forget
Now that I have turned into you
There is no safe place.

Friendships that stood the test

Less and less has been spoken
Of friendships that stood the test of time
Where are the thank yous for the friends that
held you through your bad phase
The ones that dropped their schedules for your
sorrows
The friends who lessened your pain with their
presence
The shoulders you cried on
The ones that drank like pirates by your side
As you wept and wailed
The ones whose loyalty can't be compared
To any lover
Past, present or future
Where is the shoutout

To the friendships that kept you going
To the friendships that kept you alive.

29

I wish you a river of love

If I could wish you
A love
For a lifetime
I would not wish you a passionate fire that
ignites your bones
Nor would I wish you a slow burn that warms
you slowly
I would wish you a steady flow of appreciation
and gratitude
The kindness and gentle yet consistent stream of
love and passion directed your way
I would wish you a river
A love that cuts through the challenges and finds
its way
Not fire that burns your candle on both ends
Or weakens your bones from igniting them too
fast or too long
I would wish you a river
To take you across the toughest path
In a gentle childlike manner

I would wish you a river to nourish your
attention, your wants and desires
A river, so nothing goes up in flames
A river, so you sail through life smoothly
I wish you a river of love.

What about love

Our mortal cloth
Has a series of wants and desires
Unlocked like a game with infinite levels
You never have enough
You never do enough
You race against time
You pace fast and slow
Argue, settle and repeat
You find what's good on paper
You dream of what's good in bed
You tirelessly chase goals and ask what's next
You move mountains
You work through sleepless nights
You walk, run and fly to the next thing
Until you die
What about love?

Open wounds

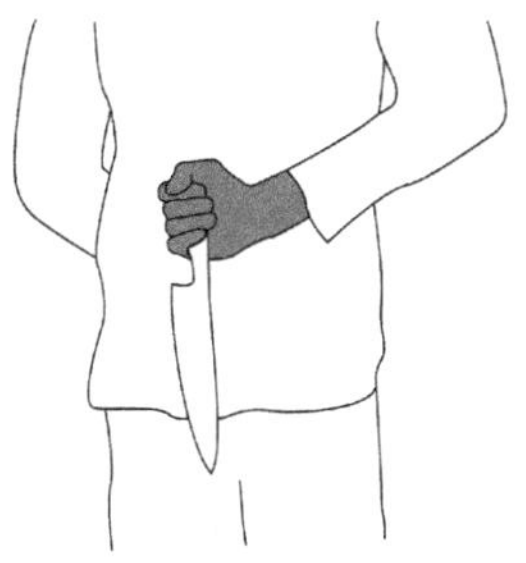

Pink and raw
Like paper cuts
Pieces of a broken heart
She hides her open wounds
Behind smiles
Behind stolen glances at happy couples
Behind big black sunglasses
Her hair falls on her face
Trying to hide the disappointment, the longing
Open wounds hurt
Deeper than the rest
She tries her best
She hides
Open wounds.

Is love the ocean?

Is love the ocean?
It invites you, lures you in
Cradles you in its waves
Much of it is uncharted, untouched
It comes in giant waves
Most of all
It consumes you
Your body and spirit
It asks you
To surrender
And feel
The sun in your face
The water on your skin
The life inside you
It makes every inch of you
Feel more alive.

Chase her

Chase
And she runs faster than ever before
Neediness drives her away
A lone wolf is who she's drawn to
Not a man, not a lover
A selfish beast
Call it alpha, leader of the pack
The one who stands the tallest
The fastest and bravest of them all
When he has her fill
He moves on
To the next one they are chasing
And for her
The chase begins
Now she chases the admirers long gone
The lovers who no longer queue in admiration

Chase her when she's looking to be chased
Catch her when the spotlight is gone
For when you hold her in a trust fall
She'll rise to her best form yet
She'll shine brighter than the stars
If you chase her
And hold her
When she falls.

You walked away

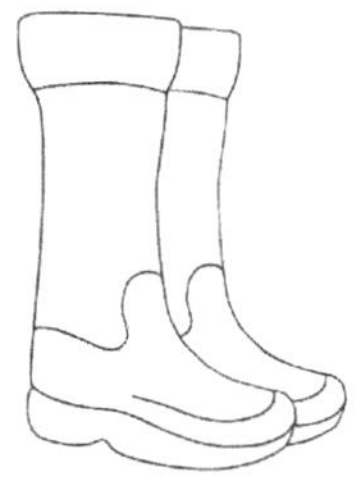

You walked away
Yet never left
I close my eyes
And you're right here
Lounging in your favorite chair
Humming my favorite song
I taste you on my salty lips
As I stare at the sea
You're the wind in my hair
My cozy sweater smells of you
Just as my bedsheets do

Can you tell me why you walked away?
Did you never intend to stay?

What do you love for

I love
So I can feel my heart beat
Outside me
In another chest.
What do you love for?

What if

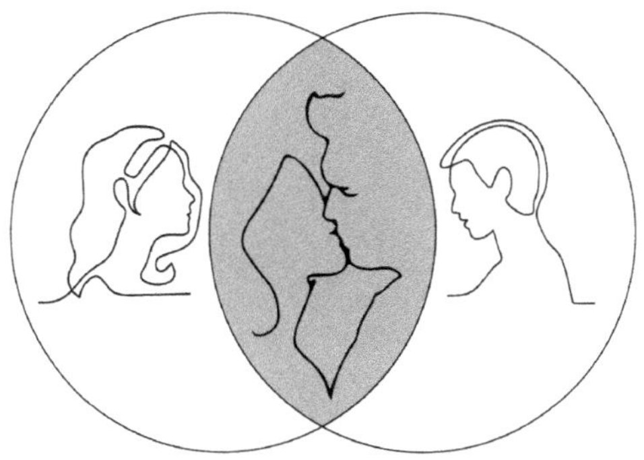

What if there is no end
To a lifetime of U-turns
Wrong exits
Missed stops
What if there is no destination
What if the journey is all you get?

Lost

In a sea of people
That come and go
I am
Held
Loved
Missed
Remembered
And yet
I keep waiting
To be found…

Pieces

You may not have
The whole of me
And yet
You hold a piece
Everytime you love someone
You collect a piece of them
A mosaic of love
If you will

Pieces of me
Find themselves scattered
Across the world
Wherever my lovers go
I go
In pieces.

Make me feel

You make me feel in the moment
Aware
Awash with emotion

You make me feel
Real
Human
Alive
Warm
Happy
Safe

A new feeling
A million feelings at once
You make me feel
Love.

Labels

Do we need one?
No
We are good he says
Just as the sun bleeds into the sea
Part evening part night
There's no name
For my favorite part of the day
Why would we need a label anyway?

Her body is a canvas

Some painted their love
With brushes of praises
Strokes of passion, admiration
Some left blank spaces
While some
Painted it red
Expressed their anger
Broke down the canvas with the pain of betrayal
Battered it with criticism
The one who stitched the torn canvas
And loved it for its beauty and uniqueness
He came alone and in the end
She did not give up on love
She became it

Her body is a canvas
He expresses his love and adulation for it

Respects all that it has endured
Honors it for its ability
To turn love into life, and little humans
Filled with hope and light.

Have we met

As I walk by you
You smile at me
The corners of your eyes
Fill with light
And turn a little crooked
Expressing contentment
In one look
I notice the outline of your mouth
The way your face brightens up as you look at
me
You say hello
And it's all so familiar
A deep sense of déjà vu
Have we met before?
I feel like I've known you
And I've loved for
For a few lifetimes if not more.

Silent screams

When was the last time you heard the sound
Of a silent heartbreak?
Sobs silenced in the dark of the night
Despair swallowed, like a lump in the throat
When was the last time you heard
A silent scream
They are all around us
The people lost like lonely ships
In the dark of the night
Waiting for a lighthouse
Waiting for you to respond
To silent screams.

The wrong ship

You don't have to burn yourself brightly
To light up the lives of those
That give you crumbs of affection
Whose loyalty and love come and go like waves
Don't be a lighthouse
For the wrong ship.

Back to life

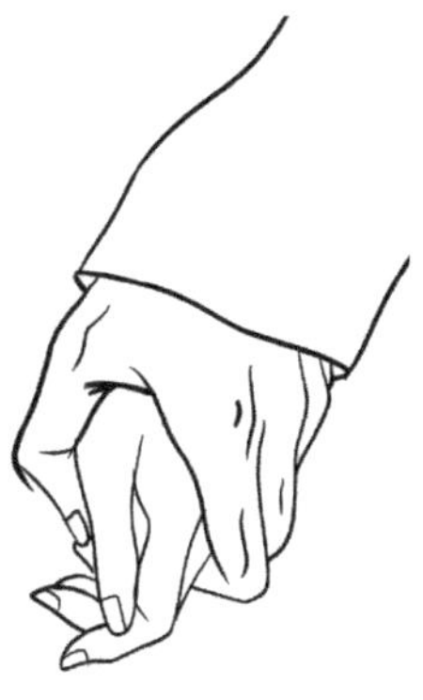

If we can move mountains
With sheer will
Bend rivers
Make it rain
If we can drill holes in the earth
Deep enough to hit the core
Why can't we
Cry a loved one back to life
Why can't we shout a name loud enough
To awaken them once again
The thought of crying you back to life
Keeps me awake at night.

Healing

Just as you let the pain
Wash all over you
Every breakup
Every heartbreak
Give healing a chance too
Let the sunshine soak into your bones
Fill every crack in your heart
Fill every teardrop with light
Let your pain marinate in the moonlight
Let it seep into your soul
Wash away the despair
Plant new seeds of hope
Let healing in
Let it begin.

Slow burn

Love at first sight
Sparks flying
Butterflies in the stomach
This may not be everyone's story
Sometimes
Love is slow
It grows on you
As you nourish it
You fulfill its every need
Sometimes
You plant roses in your garden of love
Care for it and nurture a dozen of them
Till you find the right one
To give them to
Sometimes
Love is a slow burn.

Fernweh

Fernweh they say
Is the desire
The ache to travel to distant places
What would you call the ache
To travel to distant places for a lover
For a relationship that is likely to stand the test
of time
The ache to keep looking
For the familiar face in a sea of strangers
The ache to hold on
When everyone expects you to let go
A fernweh for you.

Wayfarer

Wayfarer, would you care to spend a while
Watch a sunset
Drink some wine without a care in the world
Wayfarer, would you walk with me a mile
Make me remember what it's like to dream big
What it's like to take the lesser-known path
Remind me what it's like to renounce sleep, and
talk all night
Take my hand and let me show you
The Orange and Purple Skies.

Drown

Would you drown
Before you can swim?
Drown to live
Drown to fly
Drown before you can dream?
For success is promised to those
Willing to drown
And give up all they know
All that feels safe
Will you drown with me
For once your head is back above the water
You will never drown again.

Remarkable

Was he a ten
Why would you cry over him
Was he irreplaceable
One in a million?
They ask
What he was
Was beyond aesthetics and looks
He was a gentleman
Astoundingly soft-spoken, well-read
A man of values and high morals
A remarkable human being
Kind and memorable
And he is missed
More than I imagined was possible
He was remarkable.

Run

I run away from lies
From the fog of betrayal
That blinds my eyes
I run away from lovers
I run away in disguise
Like a dark horse
That's smitten
With the beauty of escape
The freedom it promises
The pain it numbs
I run as fast as I can
From who I have become
In your absence
Afraid of who I'll be
When you never return
Am I running towards who I want to be
Or running away from who you were

I'll never know
I run to forget it all.

Lonely without a home

When did I start turning
People into homes
The familiarity of a cologne
The safety of an embrace
The world melts away
When you forget your cares
And connect
Lock eyes
But homes don't lie
They don't abandon
They don't take what they need, up and leave
Homes aren't people
You are not lonely without a home
You are lonely within
Holding a warm cup of tea to your chest
Staring out the window, at the falling rain
You are alone

Not without a home
A home is what you've probably hidden away
In the corners of your mind
How mother calls your name
How father holds your hand and makes you feel
safe
How everything seems okay
When you close your eyes and think of home
Home within you.

Show them kindness

The world has been unkind
Showing their hand
Their true colors
Don't ask of them
Heroic acts
Or big expressions of love
Speak kind words
Show them trust
Show them kindness
Let the light of love and passion
Shine bright
I know you fear
Not getting love in return
But what is love
If not a game of roulette
Where you bet it all
On the red of love
Or the black of betrayal
Show them kindness, my friend
Because the world has been unkind.

Don't ask for forever

When you say forever
The best I can do as a human
Is to hold your hand
Stare into your eyes
For hours on end
Throw away the clocks
Calendars and schedules
And spend minutes, hours and days with you
I cannot promise forever
My time isn't mine
It's promised away
I don't decide
Which moment is my last
The best I can do
Is be here
Be with you now
Drop everything that occupies me
And give you my attention

Hold my gaze and tell me
If you'd do the same for me
Don't ask for forever
All I have is now.

Show me the skies

When I pass on
To a different dimension
To the worlds unknown
And rid myself of the mortal cloth
Don't burn me
Don't build monuments of stone
Just lay me to rest
In a field of sunflowers
That gaze everyday
At the sun
Show me the clouds
The Orange and Purple Skies
Show me the rain
Let it fall all over the earth
That consumes me
And gives me new life
As a flower
A bird
Or a bee.

She fears no one

No one can stop her stride
No end to her ambition
No tear in her eyes
She is a fearless woman
She'll ride into the sunset
With no want or desire
But her confidence
And sense of worth
That needs no company
Lucky are those
She blesses with her company
Luckier even
Are the ones she chooses
To gift her time
She is a fearless woman.

2 AM friends

Back in school
We could be friends with anyone
In a heartbeat
Didn't need an introduction
Or a reason
Many of those friendships last lifetimes
And then there are adult friendships
The people you meet
In crisis, in different and difficult phases of life
When you look for loyalty, integrity and
empathy
You meet people with good energy
People who care
Friends that'll hold your hand
When the walls around you start closing in
When it rains fires
When you are in over your head
When you face your biggest demons
You find love, you deal with loss
You win and lose, and lose again

But there's someone standing next to you
Through it all
Your 2 AM friends.

Do you watch the rain

So, you're one of the rain watchers too
From the comfort of your home
You look outside the window
At the dark rain clouds
As it pours
You wonder
If the sky is crying
Shedding her tears just as you do
When you process the pain
That's bottled up
Since the last time, you truly loved
And felt love
You watch the skies and tears run down your
cheeks
Just as rain wets the empty streets

Where you see yourself hold hands with your
muse
You are one with the rain
You are in the comfort of your home
Drenched, soaked in emotion
Like it rained over you.

You

We are all made of stardust
Part mortal
Part celestial
You wonder why no one understands you
It's because you were meant to be felt
Not understood
Your moods and emotions
The way your smile shines
Through the corners of your eyes
You are everything warm
Everything bright and full of life.

Dark side of the moon

Embrace the darkness inside me
She said
He told her, he could not
For she shone brightly
Her spirit and bones
Ignited with purpose.

Tune in to life

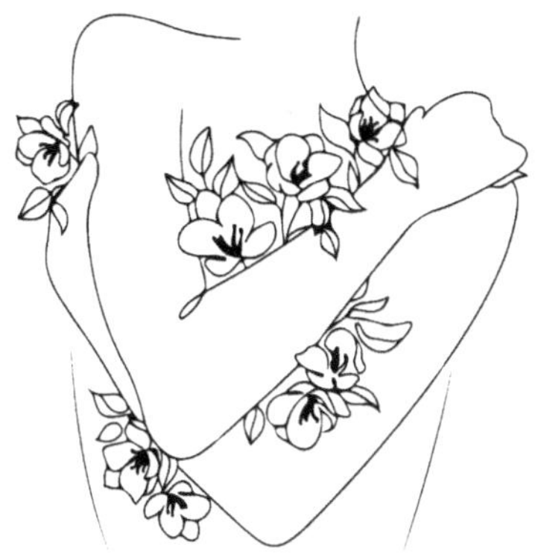

The wrong exit
An argument
A lost love
Unhappy times
Are glitches
They are noise
Once you tune in to the right frequency
You'll hear the music of life.

Distance

I often wonder how to describe
The distance between us
I think of it in terms of the breaths I draw
Without smelling your perfume
Mornings I wake up
Without kissing your face
Days that pass by
Without burying my face
In the nook in your chest
So what is distance
Distance is the time that passes
Before I can hold you again
And fill the empty space
Between us.

Love me like a song

Love me a little longer than a winter night
Like a song that fills the silences
That brings warmth to the heart
Love me but not in haste
Savor me like every bite of your favorite meal
Love me a little more
For I fear, we have less time
One lifetime may not be enough
For the connection we share
The love I hope to nurture
The four walls I wish to call home
Love me like your favorite song
Just a little longer than forever.

Charcoal and some broken glass

You said I should bring you
Evidence of my love
Rip my heart out and show you
If I'm honest
I thought of it seven days and seven nights
Through ashes and smoke
Through the heavy afternoon sunlight
Through the rain-soaked evenings
I sketched away your face on every wall of
every room I call my own
Etched your name in the corners of my heart
With shards of glass
Your love broke me
The pain was sweeter than you'd imagine
It came in waves
Washing me away

I brought you charcoal and pieces of my heart
Some broken glass
And blood-stained pages of my poetry
You looked away
You tossed it aside
Just as you did my feelings
Charcoal and some broken glass
Were evidence of many truths
We didn't find love
I found that I was lost
In a sea of emotions
A sea that you'd never swim in
Even if I drowned.

Avocado toast and wine

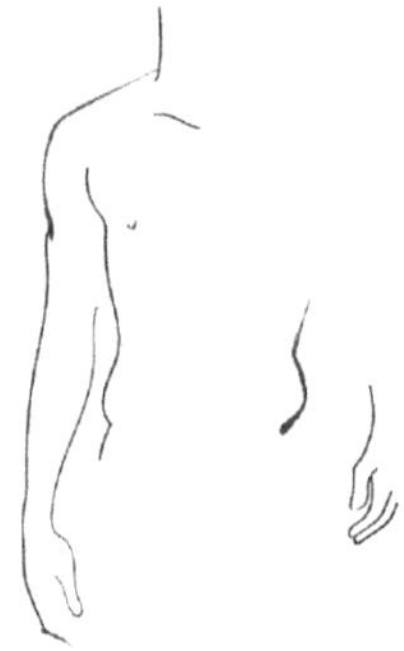

You'd wake me up every morning
To an avocado toast

You'd pour me your favorite dessert wine
You'd sing songs from the 90s
You'd talk of friendships and childhoods and
family
Of happy times spent in the company of loved
ones

You'd invite me into your home and your heart
And yet you kept me in the dark

When I found out
That this was your routine
For every woman that captures your attention
You said you didn't speak a word
Because I didn't ask

I make myself avocado toast
I pour my own wine
Everytime I engage in this ritual
It's like time travel
Takes me back to the time in my life
Where I loved your lies
Like music
I can feel you around me, almost hear your voice

All it takes is some faith, some bread and some
wine.

Mosaic of promises

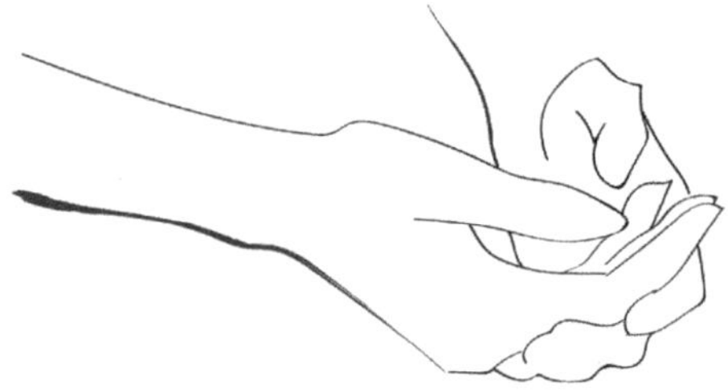

We are meant to be
Go on ahead, I'm right behind you
We are in this together
I'll be waiting right here for you
You deserve everything worth having
I'll always love you
Our love is forever
I would never give up on us
I have collected promises from lovers
Through my 20s
Putting them to good use
I created
A mosaic of promises
A wall of love I can call my own
Unrequited, fake, half-real, one-sided, lost
Complete and real
I have it all
My mosaic is all shades of love
Like a game of two truths and one lie

I swear I remember almost every story
Every fight
The warm light of love shines upon those
Who cherish being chosen
As the subject of adoration
Not once, not twice
But as many times as it takes
To meet the other piece of their soul
Another lost ship in the dark of the night.

A dream

When life feels like a dream
Even as you are awake
Alive, going about your day
With a spring in your step
You know something is right
The wheels of time have turned in your favor
Is it time?
Is it time that life becomes a dream
You've dreamt of living your entire life?
Draw a breath
Look around you
If you're in awe
You've made it
You are living a dream
Dream of a dream that fills your life with colors
you are yet to see

Dream of a dream
That is You
Fill yourself with main character energy
This dream is your life.

Do we ever forget?

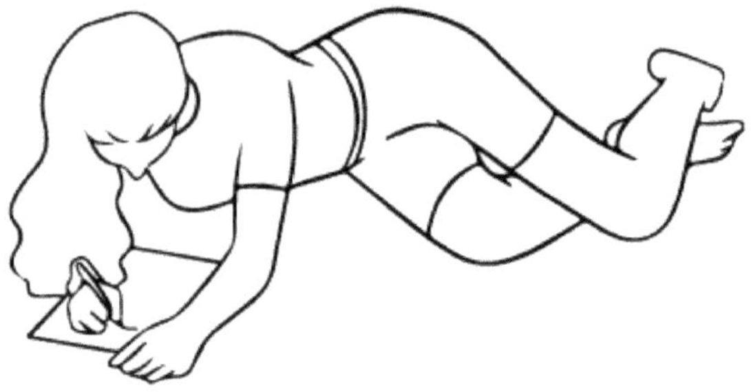

Names and places
Dates and dinners may become hazy
When your mind is clouded with memories of a
lifetime
You may think a little longer, harder
Before the face grows clearer in your head
You may not remember who it was
Or what he said
You'll remember every feeling you felt
Do we ever truly forget?

Stop

Just as you cannot stop a sneeze
Or a train that's on time
You cannot stop love
You cannot conceal the inner workings of the
heart

In stolen glances and long conversations
There is no right, no wrong
There is only a force, real and raw
It brings you together, whether you're brave or
unwilling

It demands to be felt
Choose to walk away or stay
It cannot be stopped

Fear of losing love

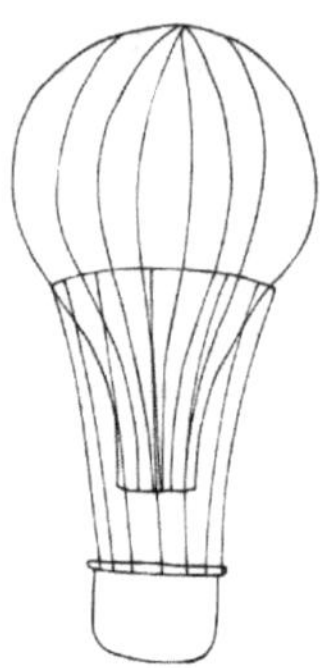

Tell me
You have felt
The fear of losing love
Even before you have it

A fear of dying alone
Wasting away
Lonely years in a lonely home

How can you fear losing something
That you don't already have?
The fear of losing love
Is the fear of losing the love you give
To a mortal capable of walking away

You fear losing a piece of your heart.

His eyes

Under a moonlit sky
Filled with stars and the glowing moon
He chooses her
To look at
His eyes filled with admiration
For a mortal being
Full of chaos, dreams and aspirations
Capable of many great things
Including love
He chooses love
He chooses her over the moon and a sky full of
stars

Years later, she stands alone and stares
At a sky full of stars
She is looking for

Admiration and love
She is looking for
His eyes.

Cracks in your heart

Maybe you meet lovers
Cruel and unkind
People who crack your heart
Leave it bruised and broken
So you can fill it with more light
And keep looking
For love
In the darkest of nights.

Little love

I don't know how to love you a little
I cannot measure it in ounces
Pour a little and put down my cup

Either I love you a lot
Or I do not

I can't keep it casual
No labels? What's that?

There is no "little love"
It's everything or nothing
Don't ask for a little love
I'd rather keep you tucked away in a corner of
my heart.

The beginning of the end

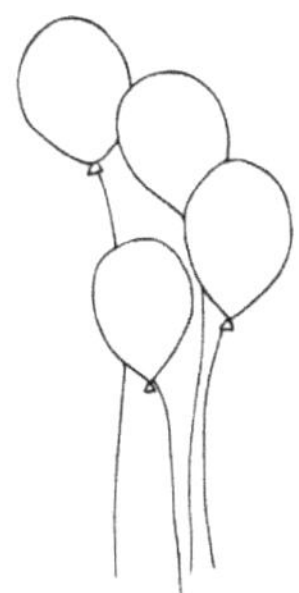

When she said yes
To jumping into the abyss
With him
It marked the beginning of the end
Of an expedition to find a lover
A species that old souls consider lost

The beginning of the end of chasing each other
It kicked off something tougher
The beginning of the end of the easy bits

Little squabbles, pet peeves
The way they disagreed
How they looked at each other, everytime the
world tried to taint the lens
Whether they came home, after every fight,
every night
It counted, it hurt, it pained

The hardest parts came later
After they found love.

Where's the time

There is love and admiration
First glances, endless texts, long calls
Click, and send, send again and again
Call and make plans, plan for plans and plan it
all
There is everything but time
Time to soak it all in
The gratitude that comes from holding their face
in your hands
Looking into their eyes
Touching foreheads
Feeling their breath on your face
Hearing their heart beat beneath your palm
As you stare at the changing colors of their eyes
in the golden hour
There is love
There is lust
There are promises and plans

Where's the time to feel the feelings?
Why is it rushed
Where's the time?

You promised me dreams

Of everything I do
I loved dreaming vividly
Every figment of my imagination would come
alive
In a dream
My escape from the gloom of monotonous life
I looked forward to dreaming every night
Until I met you
The keeper of time, of the world of dreams
You promised me dreams
Every day and every night
You promised me they'll come to life and
manifest
It broke my heart in a million pieces to find out
That nightmares are dreams too.
You served me a nightmare night after night
Day after day and fight after fight
You took my light away
You pushed me into the abyss

You crushed my imagination with a tight grip of
terror
Why did you promise me dreams?

Die once, or die twice

Would you rather let it rain fire
Or wait for the world to freeze over
Before you realize
That I'd stand with you through it all, he said
What difference does it make, I ask
Everything, he said
If you'd ask me to perish once and for all
I'll take the rain of fire
Hold your hand as it consumes us
Delivers us to worlds unknown
If you hate me enough to crush my spirit
Watch me perish, not once, but twice
I'd stay as the world freezes over
Turns my heart to ice

As the warmth of my love for you is lost in the
cold
Time would stand still
As I fall into limbo
It would be as if I lived once, and died twice.

Amateur in love

People throw around the word amateur
carelessly
As if it was a bad thing
Amateur comes from amatore
A Latin word for lover
One who does things for the love of it
Nothing less and nothing more
Let us be amateurs in love.

I am love

He didn't take a knife to my heart
His words were like a blunt blade, resilient,
repetitive
Chipping away at my love and aspirations
Bit by bit

His hands were never raised
There was no violence
No sounds of pain
Only silent screams and woes
My chest felt hollow from sadness and pain

This man didn't choose to hurt me
He chose to unlove
Take away all that he gave, in kindness and love

The crime of passion was bittersweet

I felt proud that there was once love
That he had to pull away from
Take back
Bit by bit

He was entangled, his life enmeshed with mine
The promises, kind words, loving exchanges
Fade from my memory as years pass

There is sunshine behind every dark cloud
The crime of passion is a sign that there was
once love

The realization is dear to me
For I was not a fool, I didn't dream it
I lived it …

I was loved
I loved…

I am love.

About the author

Ekta Mourya is an Indian poet, artist and author. Born in Mumbai, Mourya took interest in poetry and spoken word as early as the age of four.

She wrote her first poem as a gift for her mother in the year 2000.

'Orange and Purple Skies' is her first poetry collection featuring heartfelt words, letters, and poems inspired by friendship, love and the warmth of human relationships.